# OUT OF THE BLUE

A JOURNAL FOR FINDING YOUR WAY
FROM DEPRESSION TO HAPPINESS

NADIA HAYES

CASTLE POINT BOOKS
NEW YORK

www.castlepointbooks.com

The Castle Point Books trademark is owned by Castle Point Publishing, LLC.
Castle Point books are published and distributed by St. Martin's Press.

ISBN 978-1-250-27059-7 (trade paperback)

Design by Tara Long

Images used under license from Shutterstock.com

Our books may be purchased in bulk for promotional, educational,
or business use. Please contact your local bookseller or the Macmillan
Corporate and Premium Sales Department at 1-800-221-7945, extension 5442,
or by email at MacmillanSpecialMarkets@macmillan.com.

First Edition: 2020

10 9 8 7 6 5 4 3 2 1

# THIS BOOK BELONGS TO:

Sunflower

# INTRODUCTION

**OUR ROADS iN LiFE ARE PAVED WiTH A RAiNBOW OF
EMOTiONS.** Whether you're passing through a shade of
blue or dealing with an extended stay, you will find paths
to brighter days in *Out of the Blue*. Thoughtful prompts and
creative exercises go beyond trying to cheer you up, offering
instead space to understand and to sit with your current
feelings. Each page gets you ready to move forward and to
turn the corner to a more naturally positive mindset. Discover
new perspectives and explore proven strategies that can
help you any time you feel the blues.

As you spend time with the pages of this guided journal,
you'll begin to break free from conventional notions of
what a happy life should look like and to reclaim true
happiness and meaning. Day by day, you'll reconnect with
joy, purpose, gratitude, beauty, and mindfulness, all within
simple moments of your life. Your first entry is your first step
out of the blue.

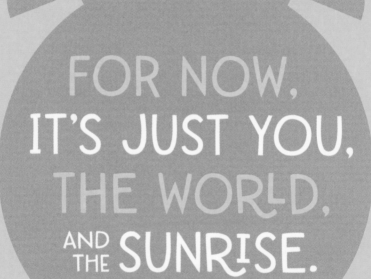

FOR NOW, IT'S JUST YOU, THE WORLD, AND THE SUNRISE.

—UNKNOWN

# CREATE MORNING MAGIC

The first few minutes after waking can set the tone for the day.
Plan a few simple ways to turn the dial toward joy.
What wake-up song or alarm sound will rouse you with a smile?

I have early riser in
my apple it helps
me start my day pleasant.

From fresh flowers to a favorite photo,
what will you place so that it's your first sight?

What simple action will energize you before your feet even hit the floor—
maybe stretching or spending a few minutes in meditation or prayer?

# FIND PURPOSE IN TOUGH TIMES

What big or little rough patch are you going through?
Describe the circumstances and the emotions involved.

........................................................................

........................................................................

........................................................................

........................................................................

........................................................................

........................................................................

........................................................................

Now, think about what the experience could be building within you.
Circle and focus on the positive words that connect with you.

FAITH

RESILIENCE

EMPATHY

CONNECTIONS

STRENGTH

COPING SKILLS

WE ARE ALL
IN THE GUTTER,
BUT SOME OF US
ARE LOOKING AT
THE STARS.

—OSCAR WILDE

# THERE ARE ALWAYS FLOWERS FOR THOSE WHO WANT TO SEE THEM.

—HENRI MATISSE

# SEEK BEAUTY WHEREVER YOU GO

In two places you find yourself throughout your day, look around for at least one sight you consider beautiful. Is it something you have always appreciated, or did you just notice it for the first time today? Sketch and write about what you see.

LOCATION #1 ........................................

LOCATION #2 ........................................

# CHOOSE YOUR PATH

List three choices that are completely within your control today. They may be as simple as what you'll wear, what you'll eat, how you'll get from point A to point B, or how you'll spend pockets of free time. For each, plan how you will make a choice that brings you joy.

1

2

3

# THE RIGHT TO CHOOSE YOUR OWN PATH IS A SACRED PRIVILEGE. USE IT.

—OPRAH WINFREY

THE REAL VOYAGE
OF DISCOVERY
CONSISTS NOT
IN SEEKING NEW
LANDSCAPES BUT IN
HAVING NEW EYES.

—MARCEL PROUST

# TRY A NEW VIEW

Take a photo, zooming in as much as your lens allows—even
if the subject gets blurry. How does the actual object differ
from what you see in the photo? Would someone else be able
to guess what the object is, based on your photo?

Is there any situation in your life you may need
to step back from to gain new perspective?

# DRiNK IN EVERY DAY

What are you thirsty for more of in your everyday life? Circle the words
that resonate with you, or add some of your own.

FUN

ADVENTURE

HARMONY

COMPANIONSHIP

FRESH AiR

CREATiVE PURSUiTS

INTELLECTUAL CHALLENGE

What small step can you take this week to quench that thirst?

ALWAYS BE
THIRSTY
FOR LIFE;
ALWAYS BE
HUNGRY
FOR LOVE.

—DEBASISH MRIDHA

MUSIC IN THE
SOUL CAN BE
HEARD BY THE
UNIVERSE.

—LAO TZU

# HEAR THE MUSIC

Think of your thoughts as music today. Sometimes they are
pulsing party beats; other times they are a melancholy ballad.
They do not define you, but they do set the tone of your daily
life if you let them. Listen to the music of your thoughts
right now and describe how they sound below.

# MAKE YOUR FIRST MOVE

What mountain is weighing heavily on your mind and mood this week?
Name it below.

Now sketch and label three smaller stones that you can reasonably
clear away as first steps toward freedom and joy.

# THE MAN WHO REMOVES A MOUNTAIN BEGINS BY CARRYING AWAY SMALL STONES.

—CHINESE PROVERB

LIFE IS A TRAIN OF MOODS
LIKE A STRING OF BEADS,
AND AS WE PASS THROUGH
THEM, THEY PROVE TO BE
MANY-COLORED LENSES
WHICH PAINT THE WORLD
THEIR OWN HUE.

—RALPH WALDO EMERSON

# KNOW YOUR LENS

What color would you name your mood today? What circumstances or people in your life could be coloring that view?

_____

_____

_____

_____

Now name the color you would like your mood to be tomorrow. What small steps could move your mood on the color spectrum?

_____

_____

_____

_____

_____

_____

_____

# FREE YOUR CREATIVE SPIRIT

Think of a creative pursuit—maybe painting a picture,
writing a song or short story, taking dancing lessons—you've
dreamed of starting. What is stopping you?

The conditions may never be perfect for this pursuit, but consider
all the good it could bring you. Would time spent in this activity bring
you stress relief, time enjoyed with loved ones, a healthy challenge?
List the benefits below, then go for the good.

THE BEST
IS THE
ENEMY OF
THE GOOD.

—VOLTAIRE

MAY YOUR CHOICES REFLECT YOUR HOPES, NOT YOUR FEARS.

—NELSON MANDELA

# CONSIDER ALL THE OUTCOMES

What event or situation coming up in your day
is worrying you most right now?

---

---

What is the worst that could happen?

---

---

What is the best that could happen?

---

---

Later, come back and record what actually did happen.
(Usually, it's somewhere in the middle of our imaginings.)

---

---

---

---

# STOP AND NOTICE

Choose a time interval—as often as every hour or spaced out
with each meal—to schedule quick joy check-ins, then set a reminder
on your watch, phone, or computer. Each time, spend just a few
minutes listing what made you smile, chuckle, or simply feel warm
inside since the last check-in. You may be surprised at the little
moments that shine through even on the seemingly worst days.

| TIME | JOYS |
| --- | --- |
| | |
| | |
| | |
| | |
| | |
| | |
| | |
| | |

MANY PEOPLE LOSE THE SMALL JOYS IN THE HOPE FOR THE BIG HAPPINESS.

—PEARL S. BUCK

# IN NATURE, NOTHING IS PERFECT AND EVERYTHING IS PERFECT.

—ALICE WALKER

# CONNECT TO NATURE

Whether you walk barefoot on grass or dip your hands
into fresh water, find a way to grasp part of nature.
How did you feel before, during, and after the experience?

BEFORE

DURING

AFTER

# FEEL THE LOVE

Think of all the affectionate names friends and family call you.
Can you remember when they first gave you the names
and the meanings in the moments? Let them replace any
negative labels others give to you or you give to yourself.

DO THE
HEART-WORK
ON THE IMAGES
IMPRISONED
WITHIN YOU.

—RAINER MARIA RILKE

I'D RATHER RIDE
A REAL HORSE
THAN WAIT FOR
AN IMAGINED
UNICORN.

—NEIL PATEL

# OPEN UP OPPORTUNITIES

What have you been waiting for that's honestly unrealistic?
How would it feel to let it go?

What very real opportunities for joy have
you let go because you were waiting?

# Name Your Retreats

We all need places where we feel secure, comfortable, refreshed. Make a list of safety zones for you. Aim for a mix of places you can duck into for 15 minutes as well as places where you can spend days.

QUICK ESCAPES                    PEACEFUL GETAWAYS

...................................          ...................................

...................................          ...................................

...................................          ...................................

...................................          ...................................

...................................          ...................................

...................................          ...................................

...................................          ...................................

Set a date when you will visit one from each column.

...................................................................................

...................................................................................

...................................................................................

NO MATTER
WHERE YOU GO,
YOU'LL BE HAPPY
AS LONG AS
YOU KNOW WHY
YOU'RE THERE.

—RACHEL KAPELKE-DALE

I THINK ONE
DAY YOU'LL FIND
THAT YOU'RE THE
HERO YOU'VE
BEEN LOOKING
FOR.

—JIMMY STEWART

# ASK FOR INSIGHT

While setting value through others' perceptions isn't always smart,
asking people you trust to recognize your gifts can be helpful.
Identify two key people in your life and write down how you think each
would describe you. Then go right to the sources and get their answers.
Do your perceptions and what they know about you match up?

PERSON

HOW I THINK THEY SEE ME

HOW THEY DESCRIBE ME

PERSON

HOW I THINK THEY SEE ME

HOW THEY DESCRIBE ME

# LOOK TO BRIGHTER DAYS

On a good day, cover this page with all the things
you can do to feel better on those hard days.

# THE TIME TO REPAIR THE ROOF
## IS WHEN THE SUN IS SHINING.

—JOHN F. KENNEDY

YOUR BODY
CAN BE YOUR
BEST FRIEND
OR WORST
ENEMY.

IT ALL
DEPENDS ON
HOW YOU
TREAT IT.

--UNKNOWN

# TREAT YOUR BODY RIGHT

There is no denying that the mind–body connection is real.
When you are feeling sad, where do you physically feel the emotion?
Color all the areas in blue.

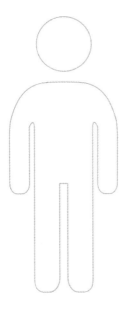

How could you relieve the sensations in those areas?

--------------------------------------------------

--------------------------------------------------

--------------------------------------------------

# HiGHLiGHT THE GOOD

Staying in touch with inspiration can help you fight the cynicism that
threatens to bring you down. Capture a few headlines from
stories of strength, courage, beauty, and kindness, and attach them
here to help you trust in, and focus on, the good that's possible.

CHOOSE TO KEEP
YOUR FOCUS ON

THAT WHICH IS
TRULY MAGNIFICENT,
BEAUTIFUL, UPLIFTING,
AND JOYFUL.

—RALPH MARSTON

BETTER A
DIAMOND
WITH A FLAW
THAN A PEBBLE
WITHOUT.

—CONFUCIUS

# CELEBRATE YOUR STRENGTH

In what areas do you often tell yourself you're a failure?
What is a more honest grade?

For every flaw you struggle with, counter with a way
your diamond strength comes through.

FLAW                                    STRENGTH

# SCAN THE RADAR

Emotions can be as unpredictable as the weather. How would
you describe your state of mind in weather terms right now?

--------------------------------

--------------------------------

--------------------------------

--------------------------------

If it's not so sunny, what's the last thing
you remember that made you feel sunny?

--------------------------------

--------------------------------

--------------------------------

--------------------------------

--------------------------------

--------------------------------

# YOU ARE THE SKY.
## EVERYTHING ELSE IS JUST THE WEATHER.

—PEMA CHÖDRÖN

ALTHOUGH I AM
HEAVY-HEARTED,
MY SPIRITS
ARE RISING.

—JEAN CRAIGHEAD GEORGE

# CLAIM THE DAY

Feeling buried by commitments? Carve out an entire day to spend any way you'd like. Make a plan or let yourself be guided completely by the moment. Capture highlights of the day and feelings of freedom in words or pictures below.

# EMBRACE YOUR CIRCLE

When you need someone to just listen or help give you a lift,
who can you turn to? Name your support system near you,
within an hour's drive, and always available by phone or text.

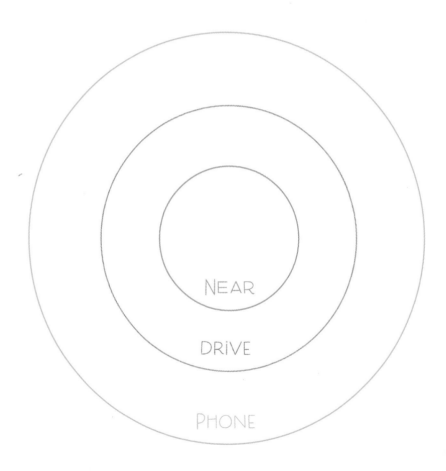

NEAR

DRIVE

PHONE

WE BUILD TOO MANY WALLS AND NOT ENOUGH BRIDGES.

—ISAAC NEWTON

HAPPINESS IS
NOT A MATTER
OF INTENSITY
BUT OF BALANCE,
ORDER, RHYTHM,
AND HARMONY.

—THOMAS MERTON

# AIM FOR BALANCE

Whether dating back to your childhood or relatively new,
what traditions in your life do you look forward to?
What steps can you take to guard them?

Are there traditions that only bring you down?
How can you release them from your life?

# FOLLOW THOSE FEELINGS

Think of a time you felt like everything was right in the world.
Where were you and what were you doing?

Can you find a way to recreate the feeling when you need a boost?

TRUST
THE VIBES
YOU GET.
ENERGY
DOESN'T LIE.

—UNKNOWN

TAKE EVERY
EXPERIENCE,
INCLUDING THE
NEGATIVE ONES,
AS MERELY STEPS
ON THE PATH.

—RAM DASS

# SEE TURNING POINTS

In what areas of your life are you at turning points, where you could choose a different, better-for-you path?

What will it take to make those turns?

# BREATHE IN HAPPINESS

Some of our strongest emotional responses are tied to scent.
What scents conjure up pleasant feelings for you?

SCENT

CONNECTED MEMORY


FEELINGS IT BRINGS


SCENT

CONNECTED MEMORY


FEELINGS IT BRINGS


SCENT

CONNECTED MEMORY


FEELINGS IT BRINGS

# BREATHE, IT'S JUST A BAD DAY, NOT A BAD LIFE.

—UNKNOWN

# I TIE NO WEIGHTS TO MY ANKLES.

—C. JOYBELL C.

# RELEASE IT ALL

Is there a truth or an emotion you've been holding in?
Release it—and all the associated weight—below.

How do you feel after letting it out? Does it need
to go beyond these pages to help you heal?

# MOVE YOUR MOOD

Physical movement boosts your mood and energizes your body.
Look at your week ahead and plan at least one activity
each day that gets you moving, even if it's just a leisurely stroll
or some crazy dancing in your kitchen.

MONDAY

TUESDAY

WEDNESDAY

THURSDAY

FRIDAY

SATURDAY

SUNDAY

When you reach the end of the week, note how you
feel and which choices brought you the most joy.

TRUE ENJOYMENT
COMES FROM ACTIVITY
OF THE MIND AND
EXERCISE OF THE BODY;
THE TWO ARE
EVER UNITED.

—ALEXANDER VON HUMBOLDT

LEARN FROM
YESTERDAY,

LIVE FOR
TODAY,

HOPE FOR
TOMORROW.

—ALBERT EINSTEIN

# FOCUS ON POSSIBILITIES

Fill this page with all the good things that are likely to happen
in the next week. They can be as as simple as...Will you enjoy
a cup of coffee each day? Connect with a friend? Feel the sun
on your skin? Expect good things to happen each day.

When you reach the end of the week, note how you feel
and which choices brought you the most joy.

# CLEAR AWAY THE MESS

Choose one physical place in your life to clean up and organize.
It could be as small as your junk drawer or bureau surface. Or
maybe you can commit to making your bed each day when it's not
a usual habit. In words or pictures, document a before and after.

BEFORE                          AFTER

How do your mind and emotions feel after the cleanup?

KEEP
YOUR MIND
AS BRIGHT
AND CLEAR
AS THE
VAST SKY.

—MORIHEI UESHIBA

To be happy,
set a goal that
commands your
thoughts, liberates
your energy,
and inspires
your hopes.

—ANDREW CARNEGIE

# EYE A PRIZE

Having a clear goal to strive for can help you feel more optimistic and in control. What goals can you easily achieve in the next month?

What loftier but still reasonable goals can you set for the next year?

Are there unrealistic goals that are becoming burdens that you need to release?

# ADJUST YOUR FOCUS

What event or situation coming up in your day
is worrying you most right now?

---

---

---

---

---

---

If a loved one were confiding this worry to you,
what advice would you give them?

---

---

---

---

---

SOME PEOPLE ARE
ALWAYS GRUMBLING
BECAUSE ROSES
HAVE THORNS;
I AM THANKFUL
THAT THORNS
HAVE ROSES.

—JEAN-BAPTISTE ALPHONSE KARR

CHILDREN
SEE MAGIC
BECAUSE THEY
LOOK FOR IT.

—CHRISTOPHER MOORE

## ☀ RECAPTURE THE MAGIC

What brought you comfort and happiness when you were a child? Did you have a special blanket or lovey? Did you grab your crayons to color? Did you spend hours shooting baskets? Recall what made everything feel better and consider whether you need a version of it back in your life.

## ☀ LOOK FOR INSPIRATION

Find a photo in which you're smiling or laughing (not posed).
Attach it below and recall what you were doing and with
whom you were spending time. Make a plan to do that thing
or to connect with those people this week.

# CHOOSE JOY
## AND KEEP
## CHOOSING IT
## EVERY DAY.

—HENRI NOUWEN

THE WORLD
IS GIVING
YOU ANSWERS
EACH DAY.
LEARN TO LISTEN.

—UNKNOWN

# LiSTEN TO LiFE

Wherever you are, be very still and simply listen.
What sounds do your hear that

...make you smile?

...let you know that life is all around you?

...bring back a happy memory?

...give you an idea for something you'd like to do?

# TURN TO WORDS

What words make you think "wow" or fill you with hope?
Letter them artfully here.

Words you've read:

Lyrics from a song:

Advice from a loved one:

# THERE'S A POWER IN WORDS.

—TRACY CHAPMAN

LET LIFE
LIVE THROUGH
YOU.
—RUMI

# GET PAST RUTS

Routines are healthy until they turn into ruts. Are you in a place where every day feels stuck on repeat? All throughout your day, look for different turns you can take—what you eat, what you wear, the music you listen to, how you spend your 30 minutes before bed.
Record your new choices and how they made you feel. In some areas, you may go back to the usual; in others, you can forge new paths.

THE USUSAL .....................................................................................

NEW TURN ......................................................................................

HOW IT FELT ...................................................................................


THE USUSAL .....................................................................................

NEW TURN ......................................................................................

HOW IT FELT ...................................................................................


THE USUSAL .....................................................................................

NEW TURN ......................................................................................

HOW IT FELT ...................................................................................

DO NOT LOSE
YOUR INNER
PEACE FOR
ANYTHING
WHATSOEVER,
EVEN IF YOUR
WHOLE WORLD
SEEMS UPSET.

--SAINT FRANCIS DE SALES

# CLEANSE YOUR FEED

The daily voices in our lives are powerful in shaping our mood—even when they're contained on a screen. What social media accounts and connections put you in a better mood and lend good perspective?

Which ones seem to feed your blue feelings?
Can you downplay or delete them?

# PUT FEELiNGS INTO WORDS

When you're going through tough times, naming exactly how you feel can help make those feelings seem less overwhelming. Whether you're feeling sad, anxious, worried, even depressed, write the emotion in big bold letters below. Then write it a few more times, getting smaller and lighter as you move down the page. Feeling good today? Do the opposite and write the positive emotion in increasingly larger, bolder letters.

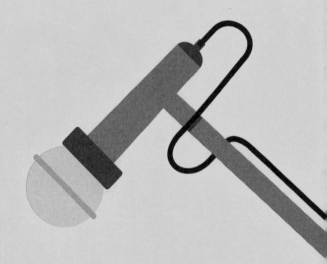

THE MOST
IMPORTANT THINGS
ARE THE
HARDEST THINGS
TO SAY.

—STEPHEN KING

EVERY GIFT
FROM A FRIEND
IS A WISH FOR
YOUR HAPPINESS.

—RICHARD BACH

# APPRECIATE YOUR GIFTS

Gifts of all kinds can remind you how much others value you and all
you bring to the relationship. Relish the memory of

...the best gift you ever received.

...the last big hug you were given.

...a card or thank-you note that made you
tear up at the love communicated inside.

...a time when someone completely
surprised you with an act of kindness.

# REMEMBER WHERE YOU'VE BEEN

What struggles have you overcome? Acknowledge both
the small (an event not going the way you planned or losing
your phone) and the big (loss of a job, health, or loved one).

How does it make you feel to look back now
and realize you pulled through?

A SEED
RISES FROM
DIRT TO PROVE TO
THE WORLD THAT
ITS GREATNESS LIES
NOT ON WHAT THE
WORLD THINKS OF IT,
BUT FROM WITHIN.

—MATSHONA DHLIWAYO

YOU CAN,
YOU SHOULD,
AND IF YOU'RE
BRAVE ENOUGH
TO START,
YOU WILL.

—STEPHEN KING

# STOP THE WAITING

What small, healthy change have you been wanting to make?
Identify one little thing you can do to give each day a boost—maybe
going for a morning walk, drinking more water, texting a good friend,
or taking a 5-minute deep-breathing break. Commit to trying it for
30 days, then hold yourself accountable by checking off each
victory here. Miss a day? Don't give up—get right back on track.

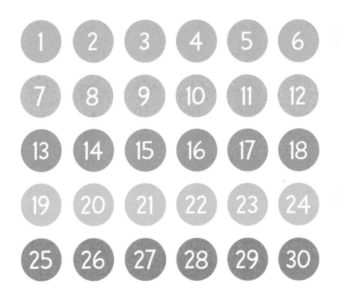

How do you feel when you hit Day 30?

_____

_____

_____

# ILLUMINATE YOUR SOUL

When you can't seem to summon any sunshine inside yourself, in what places can you feel the warmth of the sun? Think of places outdoors as well as within your home and workspace.

How can you add more light of all kinds to your spaces?

LIVE IN
THE SUNSHINE,
SWIM IN THE SEA,
DRINK THE
WILD AIR.
—RALPH WALDO EMERSON

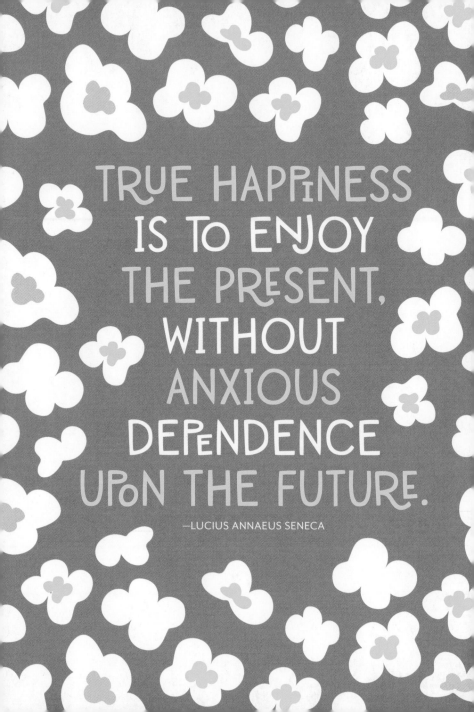

TRUE HAPPINESS
IS TO ENJOY
THE PRESENT,
WITHOUT
ANXIOUS
DEPENDENCE
UPON THE FUTURE.

—LUCIUS ANNAEUS SENECA

# CUE SCREEN THERAPY

What movie can always make you smile?
If you don't own a copy, order it now.

Describe your favorite scene and what you love about it.

# SET YOUR ANCHORS

Whether it's getting out the door in the morning, surviving
a stressful commute, or facing an evening when your mind
tends to race, define the parts of the day that are the toughest
emotionally for you. For each point, match a calming object or
activity that can enter your mental space and bring you joy.
It could be as simple as looking at a photo of a loved one.

TOUGH MOMENTS                    JOY ANCHOR

........................................    ........................................

........................................    ........................................

........................................    ........................................

........................................    ........................................

........................................    ........................................

........................................    ........................................

........................................    ........................................

........................................    ........................................

........................................    ........................................

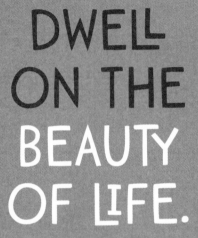

DWELL
ON THE
BEAUTY
OF LIFE.
—MARCUS AURELIUS

PEACE, HAPPINESS, AND JOY ARE POSSIBLE DURING THE TIME I DRINK MY TEA.

—THÍCH NHẤT HẠNH

# TASTE THE GOOD

Choose your favorite hot beverage to drink mindfully.
As you take each sip, imagine you are tasting all the
good things in your life right now. Record each below.

# FEEL YOUR SOUNDTRACK

Listen to a favorite sad song. What song did you choose,
and what emotions and images did it bring to the surface?

Now listen to a favorite happy song. What song did you choose, and
what emotions and images did this selection bring to the surface?

Which song felt more in sync with what you needed today?

MUSIC EXPRESSES
THAT WHICH
CANNOT BE PUT INTO
WORDS AND THAT
WHICH CANNOT
REMAIN SILENT.

—VICTOR HUGO

# TOUCH HAS A MEMORY.

—JOHN KEATS

# HOLD ON TO HAPPINESS

From furry pets to silky sheets, what can you hold or touch
that brings you joy? Make a list and look for ways to
incorporate the physical connections into your day.

# READ YOUR HEART

Sit quietly, breathe fully, and count your breaths. Keep focusing on your breaths until they slow. When you begin to feel a calmness set in, place your hand over your heart. Without overthinking or analyzing, write down whatever words or messages you feel coming from deep in your heart.

THE BEST AND
MOST BEAUTIFUL
THINGS . . .
MUST BE FELT IN
THE HEART.

—HELEN KELLER

# HEAL WiTH HELP

Who can you count on to always make you smile? Remember three
times this person ran to your side and pulled you up.

1 ........................................................................................................

.........................................................................................................

.........................................................................................................

2 ........................................................................................................

.........................................................................................................

.........................................................................................................

3 ........................................................................................................

.........................................................................................................

.........................................................................................................

IF I KNOW
WHAT LOVE IS,
IT IS BECAUSE
OF YOU.

—HERMAN HESSE

BE WILLING
TO BE A
BEGINNER
EVERY SINGLE
MORNING.
—MEISTER ECKHART

# ☀ MAKE A FRESH START

What regrets or worries are you holding on to from the past week?
Dump them here.

---

---

---

---

---

Now erase or cross out those thoughts.
How can you make a fresh start in those areas?

---

---

---

---

---

---

# GET HANDS-ON

Whether a loaf of bread, a knit scarf, or beautiful music,
making something with your hands can occupy your
racing mind and give your mood a boost. Just focus on the
process, not the outcome. What can you dig into this week?

# THE HAND EXPRESSES WHAT THE HEART ALREADY KNOWS.

—SAMUEL MOCKBEE

# TO LOVE ONESELF IS THE BEGINNING OF A LIFELONG ROMANCE.

—OSCAR WILDE

# HONOR YOUR WORTH

Without editing or evaluating, spend a few minutes
capturing all the things you appreciate about yourself.
They can be qualities like "I am loyal friend" or everyday skills like
"I pay bills on time." Whatever feels right to you is of worth.

Now, capture a few things you are glad do *not* describe you.

# COLLECT ENCOURAGEMENT

Gather up emails, thank-you notes, greeting cards, social media shout-outs, professional endorsements or letters of recommendation, and any other feedback or nuggets that remind you how amazing you are. Store them in a folder or memory box you can turn to when you need a boost.

What words from the collection are most powerful to you?

What words are most surprising when you revisit them?

I'M PROUD OF YOU.
I HOPE THAT
YOU ARE PROUD
OF YOU TOO.

—FRED ROGERS

TRULY HAPPY
MEMORIES
ALWAYS LIVE ON,
SHINING.

—BANANA YOSHIMOTO

## ☀ DRAW FROM MEMORIES

If you could return to any day of your life so far and relive it one more time from start to finish, which day would you choose, and why?

What elements of that day do you think made it so special? Can you bring them into your present life in any way?

# GIVE YOURSELF A GIFT

Find something simple in your daily travels that sparks a feeling of happiness in you. Carry it with you as a reminder that life is a wonderful journey filled with beautiful things to discover. What did you choose? Draw or describe it.

What drew you to this gift and how does it make you feel?

# LET US COME ALIVE TO THE SPLENDOR THAT IS ALL AROUND US.

—THOMAS MERTON

# TAKE TIME TO MAKE YOUR SOUL HAPPY.

—UNKNOWN

# ☀ MAKE SPACE FOR JOY

Below, create your exhaustive to-do list for the day.

Now go back and cross off at least one item that is not really necessary when you're honest. Replace it with an activity that will put a smile on your face—and make sure it gets checked off.

# TAKE SMALL STEPS

Notice the areas of your life that are improving—not perfect,
but moving in the right direction, no matter how slowly.
Draw an arrow pointing to the right next to each.

MOOD

HEALTH

RELATIONSHIPS

CREATIVITY

SENSE OF PURPOSE

WORK

FINANCES

FUN

GIVING BACK

# BELIEVE YOU CAN AND YOU'RE HALFWAY THERE.

—THEODORE ROOSEVELT

# KNOW WHAT'S IN YOUR CONTROL

Make a list of all the thoughts causing you to feel blue right now.

Now cross out the ones over which you honestly have no,
or very little, control. Then, make a new list of the ways you
could bring joy into your life or someone else's life this week.

Put a star next to the ones you're resolved to make happen ASAP.

WE CANNOT CURE
THE WORLD
OF SORROWS,
BUT WE CAN
CHOOSE TO
LIVE IN JOY.

—JOSEPH CAMPBELL

# DO A DAILY CHECK-IN

Whenever you find yourself stuck in a blue period, revisit the pages of this journal. You can also simply ask yourself: Today, how was I kind to

...MY MIND?

...MY BODY?

...MY SOUL?